Understanding Your Emotions

Joyce
Marie
Smith

Understanding Your Emotions

TYNDALE HOUSE PUBLISHERS, INC.
Wheaton, Illinois

Unless otherwise noted, all Scripture quoted is from
the *New American Standard Bible,*
© The Lockman Foundation, La Habra, California.
Used by permission.
Understanding Your Emotions.
Library of Congress Catalog Card Number 77-080737.
ISBN 0-8423-7770-0, paper.
Copyright © 1977 by Tyndale House Publishers, Inc.,
Wheaton, Illinois.
Printed in the United States of America.

94   93   92   91

30   29   28   27   26

To the precious women at "Study 'n Share"
for their inspiration and sharing of themselves.

Contents

Preface

Do your emotions control you, or do you control your emotions? There are no pat answers or shortcuts to total control over our emotions. However, as Christian women, we can daily choose our reactions to life and our relationships with others.

This Bible Study is not intended to be a psychiatrist's handbook. It is simply designed to help women examine and evaluate their emotions and feelings, and then apply some biblical principles in order to experience a more fruitful and satisfying life.

Suggestions for the Leader

Self-Preparation

1. Spend adequate time preparing your own lesson. Try to read some of the recommended books.
2. Before leading your class, ask God to cleanse you of sin. Then ask to be filled and controlled by the Holy Spirit.

Guiding the Discussion

1. Pray for sensitivity to each woman's needs, and for a genuine love for each one there.
2. A few don'ts: Don't allow tangents to develop; don't discuss controversial issues; don't get bogged down on a question that doesn't stimulate discussion; don't take advantage of the opportunity to talk excessively yourself.
3. Allow time at the end of the class for a time of prayer. Pray topically or conversationally in short, honest prayers. Keep a prayer list!
4. Encourage the women to complete their lesson each week before they come.

Femininity and Emotions:
Understanding Yourself as a Woman

Do you feel fulfilled as a woman today? Your fulfillment and stability begin when you accept your sexuality as a woman. In our study on *A Woman's Emotions* we need to understand some of our basic needs and unique characteristics.

Accepting Your Femininity

1. Do you enjoy being a woman? Why or why not? Complete the following self-evaluation.
   a. List your roles in life _____
   _____
   b. List your abilities and strengths _____
   _____
   c. List your priorities in life _____
   _____
   d. List your spiritual gifts _____
   _____

   Share with your group what you learned about yourself in a positive way.
2. Put a check by the personality/character traits that describe you:
   a. person-centered
      idea-centered

b. romantic
   practical
c. emotional and intuitive
   rational
d. security-minded
   impulsive
e. goal-oriented
   experience-oriented
f. job-oriented
   home-oriented
   (Do not be afraid to check both traits in a category.) Discuss how your image as a woman relates to each of the traits, whether as a traditional expression of femininity, or a breaking of stereotypes, or a complex combination of characteristics.

3. See Elisabeth Elliot's beautiful book, *Let Me Be a Woman*[1], which examines male/female relationships. Also, for a Bible study on the position and role of women, see *Fulfillment*.[2]

4. Dr. James Dobson discusses emotional differences between men and women in *What Wives Wish Their Husbands Knew About Women*.[3] He also shows how they differ in every cell of their bodies. As we accept and understand our emotional and physical differences, we can fulfill our feminine sexuality.

[1]Elliot, Elisabeth, *Let Me Be a Woman* (Wheaton, Ill.: Tyndale House, 1976)

[2]Smith, Joyce Marie, *Fulfillment* (Wheaton, Ill.: Tyndale House, 1975)

[3]Dobson, Dr. James, *What Wives Wish Their Husbands Knew About Women* (Wheaton, Ill.: Tyndale House, 1975), pp. 64, 65.

Understanding Yourself

5. It is important for women to understand the hormonal changes during their monthly cycle and the effect this has on them physically, emotionally, and ultimately spiritually. For further reference, see the Recommended Reading for this lesson.

   Chemical imbalance problems such as hypoglycemia also affect one's emotions.

   List other possible causes of changes in emotions and moods besides the physical. _____
   _____

6. Let's look at some varied emotions experienced by women in the Bible.

Woman	*Emotion*
a. Genesis 3:7-10	
b. Genesis 21:9-16	
c. Ruth 1:16, 17; 4:14, 15	
d. 1 Samuel 1:5, 7, 10	
e. Luke 7:37, 38	
f. Luke 10:38-42	
g. John 11:31, 32, 33	

7. List four reasons why it is important for a woman to allow the Holy Spirit to control her emotions.

   a. _____
   b. _____
   c. _____
   d. _____

8. Memorize Galatians 5:22, 23, which lists the fruit of the Holy Spirit. List three of your emotions you especially desire God to bring under his control during this course._____
   _____

   Picture yourself attaining this goal.

9. Read 1 Corinthians 13 in several versions. Ask God

15

to saturate you with his love and transform your character these coming months.

Application

1. Thank God that he made you, including your emotions, and that he understands you. Read Psalm 139.
2. Remember that your faith is based on facts (God's Word), not on your feelings (which fluctuate).
3. When you are in an emotional upheaval, depend on God's resources to give you the stability and inner calm you need.

Prayer

Father, we thank you for your many gifts to us, including our emotions. We ask that you would direct and use these gifts of feeling to help us grow, to teach us to love others, and to give glory to you. Amen.

Recommended Reading

1. Dobson, Dr. James, *What Wives Wish Their Husbands Knew About Women* (Wheaton, Ill.: Tyndale House, 1975), pp. 64, 65, 132, 133, 151-153.
2. Petersen, Evelyn and J. Allan, *For Women Only* (Wheaton, Ill.: Tyndale House, 1974), pp. 108-110.
3. Rice, Shirley, *The Christian Home* (Norfolk, Virg.: Norfolk Christian Schools, 1965), pp. 49-53.

Inferiorities:
How to Like Yourself

Many women today have an identity struggle and/or a problem with a low self-image. In fact, a low self-image is a major cause of depression in women, according to a poll taken by Dr. James Dobson.[1]

Who Are You?

1. Discuss possible reasons for a low self-image, such as:
   a. overemphasis of our culture on physical beauty or intelligence
   b. the current emphasis on the value of outside employment for women and a downgrading of housework
   c. being overshadowed by a capable, prominent husband
   d. feelings of inadequacy and inferiority rooted in childhood
   e. feelings of not being important or needed

[1]Dobson, James, *What Wives Wish Their Husbands Knew About Women* (Wheaton, Ill.: Tyndale House, 1975), p. 22.

Your Past

2. Did you feel loved as a child? Name two people who helped you feel secure and loved as a child. _____

   _____

3. Recall an experience in your childhood that made you feel inadequate, afraid, or inferior. Ask Jesus for healing of these memories and hurts. Give your past to God. (Note: Since questions 2 and 3 are highly personal, they do not have to be shared in your discussion group.)

Inferiorities or Acceptance?

4. What was Moses' attitude toward himself as found in Exodus 4:1, 10-17? _____

   _____

   Was he justified in feeling that way? _____

5. What was Paul's attitude toward himself? Summarize his attitude from these verses: Romans 12:3; 1 Corinthians 2:1-5; 1 Corinthians 15:9, 10; 2 Corinthians 12:9, 10; 2 Timothy 4:6-8. _____

   _____

   _____

   What is your impression of his balance in this area?

   _____

   Romans 12:3 reminds us to have a proper acceptance of our abilities—not overestimating or underestimating our worth, as well as accepting our limitations.

God's Valuation

6. How does God look at you? How much do you mean to God? Check these verses.
   a. John 3:16 _____
   b. Romans 8:16, 17 _____

    c. 1 Corinthians 12:27 _____

    d. Ephesians 2:10 _____

    e. 1 Peter 2:5, 9-11 _____

    You are valuable to God—he delights in you.

7. Our relationship with God and his continual gift of righteousness and forgiveness provide for the deepest needs of our self-worth and self-acceptance. A lasting sense of worth, which we cannot receive from any human being, is available each day from God.

> If your faith is in Christ, God has accepted you just as you are. To reject yourself is to reject God's grace.... Our acceptance before God gives us the security to turn repeatedly to God for strength and forgiveness. Our acceptance in Heaven gives us the basis to live here on earth.[2]

8. In 1 Peter 3:4, we find that the inner spirit is more important to God than our physical beauty. Compare Proverbs 31:30. Are you developing your inner beauty? What does God look upon? (See 1 Samuel 16:7.) _____

_____

9. Try these specific helps for improving your self-image and self-acceptance. Begin by not putting yourself down or belittling yourself in front of others. You may have to reprogram your thought patterns about yourself! Also, try these principles:

    a. Saturate yourself with God's love. Read Jeremiah 31:3; Psalm 18:19.

    b. Totally accept God's forgiveness. (See Psalm 4:1; Romans 5:1; 8:1.) Confess all past sin.

---

[2]From *Failure: The Back Door to Success,* by Erwin Lutzer, page 80. © 1975, Moody Press, Moody Bible Institute of Chicago. Used by permission.

c. You are unique and special. Thank God for the way he made you (Psalm 139:14). Ask God to help you love and accept yourself as you are.

d. Ask God for healing of your past memories and hurts (Luke 4:18).

Application

1. Did you honestly evaluate yourself and your feelings, as in questions 1-4?
2. Did you apply the principles of question 9?
3. Using your spiritual gifts for the Lord is another means of increasing your self-esteem. Are you allowing God to work through you?

Prayer

Lord, we thank you that we are "fearfully and wonderfully made." Help us to know and accept ourselves so that you can heal our inadequacies and work through our gifts. Amen.

Recommended Reading

1. Ahlem, Lloyd H., *Do I Have to Be Me?* (Glendale, Cal.: Regal Books, 1973)
2. Dobson, James, *Hide or Seek* (Old Tappan, N. J.: Fleming Revell, 1974)
3. Larson, Bruce, *The One and Only You* (Waco, Tex.: Word Books, 1974)

Lesson Three

Worry and Anxiety:
What's Your Worry?

This has been called the "Age of Anxiety" by some psychologists. As women, we may easily become consumed with worries and anxieties about finances, our children, our physical appearance, the past, the present, and the future. Our anxieties can have a very real effect on those around us.

Are You a Worrywart?

1. What are some things you worry about? _____
   _____
   _____

   How does worry differ from fear? _____
   _____
   _____

   Describe a woman you know who worries a lot. Is she an appealing person?
2. Summarize briefly these commands from the Bible regarding worry.
   a. Psalm 37:1a _____
   b. Matthew 6:25-34 _____
   c. Philippians 4:6a _____
   d. 1 Peter 5:7 _____

When you are consumed with anxiety, what are you telling God?

3. One reason God commands us not to worry or be anxious is because of the physical harm these emotions cause our bodies. John Haggai's book, *How to Win over Worry*,[1] lists many physical illnesses such as heart disorders and stomach problems which can result from worry. God wants to protect you from physical problems! Read these verses (preferably in the Amplified Version) noting the physical and emotional results of anxiety.
   a. Proverbs 12:25_____
   b. Proverbs 14:30_____
   c. Proverbs 15:13_____
   d. Proverbs 17:22_____

Battle for Your Mind

4. Worry is basically an attitude of the mind in reaction to circumstances and life. Worry and anxiety can become a habit and even begin to control our thoughts. Ultimately our thoughts affect our actions. "As he thinks within himself, so he is" (Proverbs 23:7).

   Did you know that the Bible encourages positive thinking? How does Philippians 4:6-8 encourage us to think?_____

   _____

5. Controlling our thoughts begins by realizing that we choose with our will how to think. Both Romans 8:5 and Colossians 3:2 have the phrase, "set your mind." Ephesians 4:23 says to "be renewed in the spirit of your mind."

[1]Haggai, John Edmund, *How to Win over Worry* (Grand Rapids, Mich.: Zondervan, 1959)

a. What does 2 Corinthians 10:5b say we should do with our thoughts? _____

_____

b. What result is given in Isaiah 26:3? _____

_____

6. As we yield ourselves and our thoughts to God, we can experience the control of God's Holy Spirit.
   a. What is the result of renewing our minds? See Romans 12:2: "Be _____."
   b. Galatians 5:16 says to "walk by the _____."
   c. Ephesians 5:18b says to "be filled with the ___."
   Being controlled by the Spirit on a daily basis is also an act of our will.

7. As we are controlled by the Holy Spirit, we experience victory over anxiety and other problems through Jesus Christ. Read 1 John 4:4; 5:4, 5; Philippians 4:13. Claim these promises for yourself.

Learning to Rejoice

8. Learning to rejoice is another help in overcoming habits of worry. What do these verses say about rejoicing?
   a. Psalm 34:1 _____
   b. Psalm 118:24 _____
   c. Philippians 4:4 _____
   d. 1 Thessalonians 5:16-18 _____

9. To further strengthen your faith and trust in God, find Scripture verses regarding:
   a. Promises of God, such as Deuteronomy 31:8; Isaiah 12:2; 41:10
   b. God's character

10. Now look at some of your worries listed in the first question. How significant are they after acknowledgment of who God is and what he has done?

Note: Norman Wright's book, *The Christian Use of Emotional Power,*[2] presents some very practical helps in dealing with worry and anxiety. He also discusses the area of controlling your thoughts.

Application

1. Share with your group a worry you have right now. Pray for each other.
2. Claim a verse for your cause of worry or anxiety.
3. Bring your thoughts to God and ask him to control your total self.
4. Begin to praise God for problems that cause you to trust in him alone.

Prayer

Our Heavenly Father, we bring our worries and anxieties to you. Give us release from their bondage as we seek to surrender our thoughts and emotions to your control. Amen.

Recommended Reading

1. Collins, Gary, *Overcoming Anxiety* (Santa Ana, Cal.: Vision House, 1973)
2. Osborne, Cecil, *Release from Fear and Anxiety* (Waco, Tex.: Word Books, 1976)
3. Sanchez, George, *Changing Your Thought Patterns* (Colorado Springs, Col.: Nav Press, 1975)

[2]Wright, H. Norman, *The Christian Use of Emotional Power* (Old Tappan, N. J.: Fleming Revell, 1974)

Lesson Four

Fear:
Are You Facing Your Fears?

Fear is a very real emotion in our daily lives. Fear of others can keep you from attending social functions or teaching a Sunday school class. Fear of the unknown can prevent you from taking an exciting trip because you don't want to fly. Fear of an undiagnosed disease can totally immobilize you. Fear of what might possibly happen tomorrow can easily ruin today.

Facing Our Fears

1. What are some fears you experienced as a child? __
   _____

2. List some fears you experience today, in these areas:
   a. physically _____
   _____

   b. financially _____
   _____

   c. for your husband _____
   _____

   d. for your children _____
   _____

   e. for your future _____
   _____

f. in your other relationships _____
_____

3. What are the effects of fear on you physically, socially, mentally, and spiritually?_____
_____

4. 2 Timothy 1:7 states that God has not given us the spirit of fear or timidity. When and how did fear enter the world? Read Genesis 3:1-13.
   a. Who is the agent who caused fear (v. 1)? _____
   b. What is the origin of fear (vv. 6, 7)? _____
   c. What reaction did fear bring (vv. 8-10)? _____
   Adam and Eve's basic cause of fear has been passed on to all mankind through the fallen human nature.

5. Briefly name and describe other people in the Bible who experienced fear.

	Who	*Why*
a. Numbers 13:17, 18, 26-33		
b. 1 Samuel 17:1-11		
c. 2 Chronicles 20:1-4		
d. Matthew 14:22-33		

Conquering Our Fears

6. Nehemiah and his people faced active opposition and had a valid reason to be afraid. They worked by day to rebuild the wall, and then had to guard it by night from the enemy.
   What is the reminder given to us in Nehemiah 4:14b?
   _____

   Remember, God is big enough for any problem or fear that you face.

7. List several situations in the past where God has delivered you from your problems. _____

    _____

    Thank him right now for his faithfulness in the past.
8. Read the following commands and promises of God regarding fear. Memorize your favorite verse. Share it with your group. Joshua 1:9; Psalm 16:8; 23:4; 27:1; 46:1, 2; 56:3, 11; 91:1-11; Isaiah 41:10; and 2 Timothy 1:7 (KJV).
9. In lesson 2 on worry and anxiety, we discussed: 1. controlling our minds, 2. developing a positive attitude, 3. learning to rejoice, and 4. how to strengthen our faith in God. These same principles apply to our enemy fear.

    Share with your group how one or several of these principles have been helpful to you this past week in overcoming worry or fear.

Application

1. Acknowledge your fears to God. Ask him to cleanse your mind and deliver you from these fears.
2. Ask Jesus to bring healing to memories of past experiences which caused fear.
3. Learn to depend on God. As we acknowledge God's power and our own inadequacy to handle a problem, fear will flee.
4. Is a loved one experiencing fear? Ask God to permeate this person's being with his lasting peace.

Prayer

Lord, you have the power to deliver us from our fears. Help us to depend on you and to find peace, through Jesus Christ our Savior. Amen.

Recommended Reading

1. Guder, Eileen, *Deliver Us from Fear* (Waco, Tex.: Word Books, 1976)
2. Little, L. Gilbert, *Nervous Christians* (Chicago, Ill.: Moody Press, 1956)
3. MacArthur, Jack, *How to Keep Away from the Psychiatrist* (Wheaton, Ill.: Tyndale House, 1974)

Anger:
Do You Act or React?

People react differently when angry. One woman is transformed into a screaming, yelling tyrant. Another woman holds her anger within like a smoldering volcano, as she retreats behind a cold wall of silence. Some women hold grudges and develop deep feelings of bitterness and resentment.

Blowing Up

1. Describe how you feel when you are angry. How do you react?
2. List some causes of anger in your life. _____

_____

_____

What do you think is the relationship between self-centeredness (or demanding your own "rights") and anger?_____

_____

_____

3. Sometimes you may have every *right* to be angry when someone has done something to hurt you or a loved one. Let's look at some results of anger as experienced by these Bible characters. Fill in the chart.

Person   *Cause of Anger*   *Result of Anger*

a. Genesis 4:5, 6, 8 _____

_____

b. Exodus 32:19-22 _____

_____

c. 1 Samuel 25:26, 27 _____

_____

d. Luke 10:38-42 _____

_____

4. How is an angry and contentious woman described?
   a. Proverbs 21:9_____
   b. Proverbs 21:19_____
   c. Proverbs 27:15_____
   List some effects of an angry mother and wife on her family. _____

   _____

5. What results can occur from anger (physically, emotionally, spiritually, and mentally)? Discuss this with your group. Share results of anger you have experienced. (See Proverb 10:12; 29:22; Matthew 5:22; Ephesians 4:26, 27.)

   _____

   _____

   _____

6. In Proverbs 18:6, 7, an angry person is called a fool. Read Proverbs 14:1. What does a foolish woman do to her home?_____

   _____

7. Are there ever appropriate times for anger? Define "righteous" anger. Give examples. See Jesus' example in John 2:14-17; Mark 3:5. Compare Ephesians 4:26. _____

   _____

   _____

Handling Anger

Depending on temperament, childhood experiences and models, and habits established, people generally cope with their anger by repressing, suppressing, or expressing it. In David Augsburger's excellent book, *Caring Enough to Confront,*[1] he discusses ways of expressing anger through verbal discussion and communication.

8. What advice is given regarding anger in these verses?
   a. Proverbs 15:18_____
   b. Proverbs 22:24, 25 _____
   c. Proverbs 29:11_____
   d. James 1:19 _____

   Share how you have handled anger in your own life.

Forgive and Forget

9. What are the results of an unforgiving spirit in:
   a. marriage _____
   b. parent/child relations _____
   c. friends _____
   d. relationship to God_____
10. What are some principles involved in forgiveness? See Matthew 18:21, 22; Mark 11:25, 26; and Ephesians 4:26, 30, 32. _____
    _____
11. In dealing with anger and an unforgiving spirit:
    a. Honestly confess your anger as sin to God. Ask him to cleanse and deliver you from anger (1 John 1:9). Remember, anger grieves the Holy Spirit.
    b. Forgive the other person (through God's grace and forgiveness).

[1] Augsburger, David, *Caring Enough to Confront* (Glendale, Cal.: Regal Books, 1973)

   c. If need be, ask the person to forgive you for your anger (James 5:16).

   d. Ask to be filled with love for him, and then actively show love to him.

Application

1. Begin to communicate and express verbally your feelings of anger with your husband or a friend. Discuss causes of your anger.
2. Pray for each other when you need help in controlling your anger. Ask God to flood you with his love (Romans 5:5).
3. Discuss how you can help members of your family or friends deal with their anger. Pray for them.

Prayer

Lord, work in all our relationships to help us first to *communicate* and then to *control* our anger. We know we must forgive others before asking for your forgiveness, and we do this now. Deliver us from the temptation of anger and fill us with your love. Amen.

Recommended Reading

1. Augsburger, David, *Caring Enough to Confront* (Glendale, Cal.: Regal Books, 1973)
2. Augsburger, David, *Seventy Times Seven* (Chicago, Ill.: Moody Press, 1970)
3. LaHaye, Tim, *Spirit-Controlled Temperament* (Wheaton, Ill.: Tyndale House, 1966)

Depression:
The Horrible Pit

Everyone experiences highs and lows. But many women remain in a depressed state for long periods of time. A depressed person usually has a low self-image. A woman engulfed in the pit of depression is not only unhappy personally but also makes life miserable for those around her.

1. What have been some causes of depression in your life?_____

   _____

2. Share what has helped you in overcoming times of depression.

3. Are you learning to accept and like yourself (see lesson 2)?

Out of a Horrible Pit

4. Let's look at several Bible characters who experienced times of depression.

	Person	*Cause of Depression*	*Result*
a.	Numbers 11:10-18	_____	
b.	1 Kings 19:1-8	_____	

33

    c. Jonah 4:1-11 _____

_____

    Circle the one you identify with the most.
5. What was God's solution for each man?

    a. _____

    b. _____

    c. _____

6. Summarize how these men handled their feelings of despair and discouragement.

    a. Job: Job 13:15 _____

    b. David: Psalm 40:1-4; 42:1-6, 8; 43:5 _____

_____

    c. Paul: Philippians 4:4-8, 13 _____

Hope for the Depressed

7. In lesson 3 on worry, we discussed the importance of controlling our minds and thoughts. This is especially necessary for a depressive person. Our habits and mental reactions can become deeply ingrained, but Jesus can help reprogram our thoughts and minds. Review p. 22 on the "battle for your mind."

8. Realize you are in a spiritual battle and need protection from Satan's attacks. Meditate on Christ and claim the power of his victory over death. (See Revelation 12:11; Hebrews 2:14. Claim 1 John 4:4.)

9. Selfishness is a prime characteristic of a depressive person. Thinking too much about yourself and your own problems (or being too introspective) can feed your depression.

    Romans 12:3-8 encourages us to use our spiritual gifts for the Lord. In verses 9-21, list other areas of service for the Christian. _____

_____

_____

10. Practical steps to help you experience deliverance from depression include:
   a. Look for a possible physical cause such as exhaustion or ill health first.
   b. Confess all known sin, especially self-pity and anger, and receive God's cleansing (1 John 1:9; Psalm 51:10).
   c. After confessing your sin, praise God for his victory (1 Thessalonians 5:18 and 1 John 5:14, 15).
   d. Ask to be filled with the Holy Spirit and controlled by him (Ephesians 5:18).
   e. Saturate your mind with Scripture and spend time praising God in order to prevent depression.

Application

1. *How to Win over Depression*[1] has an excellent chapter on helping your children avoid depression. If you are a parent, be aware of positive ways to help your children.
2. Did you go through the steps in question 9?
3. Ask the Lord for emotional healing if the cause of your depression is a result of suppressed anger or self-pity dating back to your childhood.

Prayer

Father, lift us from the depths of depression, as you have promised to do when we turn to you. Help us not to fall into self-pity, but rather to be positive channels for your power. Amen.

[1]LaHaye, Tim, *How to Win over Depression* (Grand Rapids, Mich.: Zondervan, 1974)

Recommended Reading

1. Dobson, Dr. James, *What Wives Wish Their Husbands Knew About Women* (Wheaton, Ill.: Tyndale House, 1975)
2. Wright, H. Norman, *The Christian Use of Emotional Power* (Old Tappan, N. J.: Fleming H. Revell, 1974)

Guilt:
Is It for Real?

Why is mankind plagued with feelings of guilt? Many feel guilty because they *are* guilty—guilty of rejecting God's work of grace in their lives. But many Christians also experience a false type of guilt as a kind of self-hate and self-punishment.

1. Share some things over which you have experienced guilt.

Guilty yet Forgiven

2. In lesson 4, we saw that Adam and Eve experienced guilt as a result of sin. What was the result of their guilt (Genesis 3:6-10)?_____

_____

What does Romans 2:14, 15 say about man's conscience? _____

_____

Romans 3:23 says, "____ have sinned." Therefore, ____ are guilty in God's sight. Our very nature demands that we be forgiven or punished.

3. Read 2 Samuel 11. Name several great sins which David knowingly committed. _____

_____

What were the consequences he later suffered as a result? _____
_____

4. From Psalm 51:2-5, 10-12; 32:2-4 describe the effects of sin and guilt on David.
physically _____
_____

mentally _____
_____

spiritually _____
_____

emotionally _____
_____

5. What is God's answer to guilt?
a. Psalm 51:2, 3, 7, 10 _____
_____

b. Psalm 32:1, 5 _____
_____

c. 1 John 1:9 _____
_____

d. 1 John 2:2 _____
_____

e. Romans 5:8-10 _____
_____

We have seen that even though God forgives us, we often must suffer the consequences of our sin. However, even these experiences can help us mature spiritually and experience God's grace.

6. David greatly sinned and displeased God, but he later was called "a man after God's own heart." This truly shows the depths of God's mercy and forgiveness. How is David used as an example in Isaiah 55:3 and Acts 13:34? _____
_____

7. Pick out one of the following verses on God's forgiveness and memorize it. Psalm 103:12; Isaiah 44:22; Hebrews 9:22; Micah 7:19; Jeremiah 31:34; 1 John 1:9.

The Guilt Trap

8. Many Christians continue to experience guilt after coming to Christ for forgiveness. If the Holy Spirit convicts you of a sin (John 16:8, 13; 14:26) confess it and ask forgiveness. Make restitution if necessary. Claim victory from condemnation (Romans 8:1, 2).

9. Who brings feelings of guilt and condemnation to the Christian? (See Revelation 12:10; Job 1:9-11.) _____

_____

Erwin Lutzer[1] has several excellent chapters on accepting God's grace and forgiveness.

10. Discuss ways of helping your children or friends experience freedom from guilt.

Application

1. God has already forgiven you your sins. Have you forgiven yourself?
2. Is your pride keeping you from experiencing deliverance from guilt?

Prayer

Lord, we thank you that there is no condemnation to those who are in Christ Jesus. We claim the freedom from guilt and sin bought by your blood. Help us to live in freedom. Amen.

[1]Lutzer, Erwin W., *Failure: The Back Door to Success* (Chicago, Ill.: Moody Press, 1975)

Recommended Reading

1. Collins, Gary, *Overcoming Anxiety* (Santa Ana, Cal.: Vision House, 1973)
2. Lindsey, Hal, *The Guilt Trip* (Grand Rapids, Mich.: Zondervan, 1972)
3. Lutzer, Erwin W., *Failure: The Back Door to Success* (Chicago, Ill.: Moody Press, 1975)

Lesson Eight

Criticism and Gossip:
Are You Bitter or Sweet?

Criticism is like a cancer spreading and infecting all parts of the body of Christ. As women, many times we find ourselves trapped in a habit of criticizing others, or even gossiping about our friends to others. How can we overcome it?

1. Think of the person you criticized most recently. Was the criticism totally valid? What purpose did it serve? Who was edified?

Your Tongue

2. Romans 2:1 says we should not judge or condemn another. In Romans 14:10 what explanation is given as to why we shouldn't be critical of others? _____
_____Compare Matthew 7:1-5.

3. In Romans 1:29, 30, the unrighteous are described as indulging in gossip and slander. What will be the end result (Romans 1:32)?
_____

4. What is the source of evil words (Matthew 12:33-37)?
_____
_____

What warning is given in verses 36, 37?_____
_____

5. Describe the power and effect of the tongue from these verses:
   a. Psalm 64:3 _____

   _____

   b. Proverbs 12:18_____

   _____

   c. Proverbs 13:3_____

   _____

   d. Proverbs 18:21_____

   _____

6. Read James 3:2-12.
   a. Describe the effect of the tongue._____

   _____

   b. Can man control his tongue? _____

   _____

   c. Which verse convicts you the most? _____

   _____

7. Read James 3:13-18.
   a. What are some results of the world's wisdom? __

   _____

   _____

   b. What do you see as some root causes of criticism and gossip in these verses?_____

   _____

   c. What are results of being controlled by God's wisdom? _____

   _____

Are You in Control?

8. How do these verses tell us to control our tongues?
   a. Psalm 34:13 _____

   _____

   b. Psalm 141:3 _____

   _____

c. Proverbs 10:14, 19 _____

_____

d. Proverbs 13:3_____

_____

9. What are some results of controlling our tongues?
   a. Proverbs 15:4, 7 _____

   _____

   b. Proverbs 12:18, 19 _____

   _____

10. A critical spirit is often caused by jealousy, envy, pride, or bitterness. Gossip and slander usually begin with a spirit of criticism and judging.

   If God has convicted you of a spirit of criticism, gossip, or other sins mentioned, confess them as sin. Ask for protection of your mind from Satan's temptations in this area. If you have slandered anyone, go and ask that person's forgiveness and repair any damage done to his character. Remember, destroying a person's reputation and character can be worse than physical harm.

Application

1. Ask God to help you accept and love others as they are.
2. Pray Psalm 141:3 or Psalm 34:13 each morning this week.
3. Thank Jesus that he wants to set you free from the sins of gossip and criticism. He can give you power over your tongue.

Prayer

Father, help us to speak the truth in love this week. Forgive our sins of gossip and criticism and renew us by your power. Amen.

Recommended Reading

1. Schlink, Basilea, *You Will Never Be the Same* (Minneapolis, Minn.: Dimension Books, 1972), chapters 8 and 38.

Jealousy:
The Green-Eyed Monster

Jealousy can ferment into seething hatred, cause broken relationships, and even result in murder. When jealousy rules one's heart, it results in strife in the home, neighborhood, business, and church.

1. Think of circumstances in which you have experienced jealousy. What effect did the jealousy have on *you* and on the relationship?

Strife and Bitterness

2. Let's look at some Scripture verses relating to jealousy.

Result of Jealousy

a. Cain: Genesis 4:3-8 _____

_____

b. Sarah: Genesis 16:4-6 _____

_____

c. Esau: Genesis 27:34-41 _____

_____

d. Saul: 1 Samuel 18:8-11 _____

_____

e. Prodigal's brother: Luke 15:25-30 _____

_____

Can you think of other Bible characters who experienced jealousy? _____

_____

3. Proverbs 14:30 in *The Living Bible* says, "A relaxed attitude lengthens a man's life; jealousy rots it away." Share with your group examples of the effects of jealousy. Don't allow a root of bitterness or jealousy to grow.

4. Jealousy essentially springs from a low self-image and inferiorities. Did you apply the principles in lesson 2?

5. Read the story of Joseph in Genesis 37.

   a. What provoked the brother's anger toward Joseph? _____

   _____

   b. What was the result of their jealousy and anger?

   _____

   c. How was the relationship restored (Genesis 45:1-8; 50:15-21)? _____

   _____

   What principles do you see here regarding jealousy? _____

   _____

6. Moses was a great servant of God. When God chose Joshua to succeed Moses and lead the Israelites into the Promised Land, Moses could have experienced jealousy. But he didn't. He didn't compare his career with Joshua's. Have you ever experienced jealousy over someone else's spiritual gifts, abilities, or career? Jealousy within the Body of Christ is ugly and destructive.

   What was John the Baptist's reaction when he was compared to Jesus (John 3:30)? _____

   _____

7. In Galatians 5:19-21 and Romans 13:13, envy is listed

as a work of the flesh. What does Galatians 5:21 say will be the end result? _____

_____

God's Answer

8. Jealousy is rooted in selfishness and greed. Find God's answer for selfishness.
   a. Romans 5:5 _____
   b. Romans 8:1-13 _____
   c. 1 Corinthians 13:4 _____
   d. Galatians 2:20 _____
   e. Galatians 5:22-24 _____
   f. Galatians 5:25 _____
9. Read Romans 5:10. It actually means we can be *delivered daily from sin's dominion in our lives*, through Jesus Christ.

Application

1. Do you have a problem with jealousy? You can be delivered daily from this sin. Ask Jesus to set you free with his power. Claim one of the verses in section 8 and pray it each day this week.
2. If jealousy has caused a broken relationship with a friend, go to that person and ask forgiveness.

Prayer

Help us to guard against jealousy by being thankful for what we have. We continue to claim your promises for deliverance from this sin. Thank you that forgiveness is available in Christ. Amen.

Pride:
An Abomination to God

Pride, in the sense of self-respect or self-esteem, is good. However, in the Bible, pride refers to conceit, arrogance, feelings of superiority, and boasting. This kind of pride can be caused by feelings of inferiority and insecurity, self-centeredness, or intellectualism.

1. Underline any of the following feelings you have experienced.
   a. You don't like to be criticized, but you tend to be critical of others.
   b. You are embarrassed by your husband (or parents, friends, children) because of his lack of education, position, or appearance.
   c. You feel your talents and gifts have not been properly recognized.
   d. If you can't be the leader of a group, you don't want to be involved.
   e. You tend to look down on others and feel you are superior.
   f. You resent someone else's superior ability or talents.
   Discuss together other ways we express pride.

2. Erwin Lutzer[1] cites pride in all its forms as the most obvious reason for failure. He shows how a fear of failure and an inferiority complex are rooted in pride. How does John describe this problem in 1 John 2:16?

_____

_____

An Abomination

3. What does God say about pride?
   a. Proverbs 6:16, 17 _____

   _____

   b. Proverbs 8:13_____

   _____

   c. Proverbs 16:5_____

   _____

   d. Proverbs 16:18_____

   _____

   e. Proverbs 21:4_____

   _____

   C. S. Lewis in *Mere Christianity*[2] calls pride the utmost evil. Pride keeps us from God.
4. Who is the originator of pride on earth?_____
   Read Isaiah 14:12-14, comparing it with Ezekiel 28:12-18. How many "I wills" do you count in Isaiah 14? _____ is pride personified.
5. From the illustration given in Luke 18:10-14, list characteristics of each man. What was the final result for each man?_____

   _____

   _____

---

[1]Lutzer, Erwin, *Failure: The Back Door to Success* (Chicago, Ill.: Moody Press, 1975), p. 40.

[2]Lewis, C. S., *Mere Christianity* (New York: The Macmillan Co., 1953), chapter 8.

Have you ever been guilty of depending on your own goodness rather than on God's grace?

Servant Spirit

6. What commands are given relating to humility and meekness?
   a. 1 Corinthians 1:31 _____
   b. 1 Timothy 6:11 _____
   c. 2 Timothy 2:25 _____
   d. Titus 3:2 _____
7. What promises are given for the humble?
   a. 2 Chronicles 7:14 _____
   b. Isaiah 57:15 _____
   c. Matthew 5:5 _____
   d. James 4:6-10 _____
   e. 1 Peter 5:5, 6 _____
8. What is Jesus' example?
   a. Matthew 11:29 _____
   b. 2 Corinthians 10:1 _____
   c. Philippians 2:5-8 _____
9. List several ways you can humble yourself (Philippians 2:7, 8). _____
   _____
10. How did Jesus become a servant to the disciples (John 13:4-17)?
    _____

    List an example, command, and promise from this passage regarding becoming a servant. _____
    _____

Application

1. Confess your pride as sin. As we come to recognize sin in our lives, we can appreciate God's grace to a greater extent.

2. Ask God to give you a servant spirit.
3. Realize Satan is tempting you with a proud spirit. Claim the protection of Ephesians 6:10-18 against his attacks.

Prayer

We confess to you our pride. Humble us before you that we may seek to serve you with gladness and singleness of heart. Amen.

Recommended Books

1. Collins, Gary, *Overcoming Anxiety* (Santa Ana, Cal.: Vision House, 1973)
2. Lewis, C. S., *Mere Christianity* (New York: The Macmillan Co., 1953), chapter 8

Selfishness and Self-pity:
Double Trouble

Selfishness has been cited as the greatest single enemy to a happy marriage. Selfishness causes strife and unhappiness in many other relationships.

Me, Myself, and I

1. Fill in the following chart.

Person	Warning–Promise
a. Mark 12:41-44	
b. Mark 10:17-22	
c. Luke 12:16-21	
d. Luke 7:41-48	

2. In 1 Timothy 6:8-10 what is described as the root of all evil? _____
   Give examples or illustrations. How would you describe someone who has this problem?_____
   _____
   _____

3. What answer does Jesus give for the problem?
   a. Matthew 6:33 _____

b. Matthew 10:38, 39 _____
　c. Mark 8:34-37 _____
　d. John 12:24-26 _____
4. Look at some biblical examples of unselfishness.

Person　　　Act

　a. Genesis 13:5-11 _____
　　_____

　b. Genesis 26:18-22 _____
　　_____

　c. 1 Samuel 1:24-28 _____
　　_____

　d. John 12:3-7 _____
　　_____

　e. Acts 2:42-47 _____
　　_____

　Can you think of other examples?
5. What are two specific changes you can make to become less selfish? _____
　_____

6. What should be our main interest and concern?
　a. 1 Corinthians 10:24 _____
　b. 2 Corinthians 5:15 _____
　c. Philippians 2:4, 21 _____
　How does this apply to your family and home? To your neighborhood or place of work?

Self-Pity

7. Focusing our thoughts on ourselves and our problems or failures encourages self-pity to develop. Describe someone you know who engages in self-pity. Do you like to be with that person?
8. The book *How to Win over Depression*[1] shows that

[1]LaHaye, Tim, *How to Win over Depression* (Grand Rapids, Mich.: Zondervan, 1974), chapters 8, 9.

54

the primary cause of depression is self-pity. Self-pity can be triggered by anger or resentment over unfair treatment, or by your adverse circumstances. What principles are forgotten when we indulge in self-pity?

a. Romans 8:28 _____

b. 1 Corinthians 10:13_____

c. Ephesians 4:30, 32 _____

d. Philippians 4:6, 7_____

e. 1 Thessalonians 5:18, 19 _____

f. James 1:2, 3_____

9. Before you can begin to overcome self-pity or self-ishness, you must recognize it as sin in God's sight.

a. Confess the self-pity and selfishness as sin and receive God's cleansing (1 John 1:9; Psalm 51:10).

b. Ask God to change your patterns of thinking and reacting.

c. Praise God for his victory (1 John 4:4; Philippians 4:13).

d. Ask to be filled with the Holy Spirit and controlled by him (Ephesians 5:18).

Application

1. Do at least two things for others this week that you do not normally do.

2. Learn to confess your self-pity immediately rather than wallowing in it.

3. How can you develop unselfishness in your children?

Prayer

Dear Lord, we thank you for your unselfishness in sending your own Son to die because of our sin. Give us the power to overcome self in our lives, and to shun self-pity. We pray with grateful hearts. Amen.

Emotional Control:
Maturity and Fruitfulness

After studying your emotions and feelings these last few months, you may be discouraged. Especially if God has convicted you of sin in your life. Rejoice! This proves you are sensitive and responsible to the work of the Holy Spirit in your life. In this final lesson we will study some basic principles of developing spiritual maturity and fruitfulness—ways to strengthen that "new nature" within you.

God's Desire

1. What is God's desire for you?
   a. John 15:16 _____
   b. Romans 8:29 _____
   c. Ephesians 4:12, 13 _____
   d. Colossians 1:28 _____
2. What provisions does God make to help us develop this maturity and fruitfulness? (In class, just summarize each group of verses, rather than looking up each one.)
   a. John 14:16, 17, 26
      John 16:13, 14 _____
      Acts 1:8

57

b. Hebrews 4:12
   2 Timothy 3:16, 17 _____
   Psalm 1:1-3
c. Romans 5:3-5
   James 1:2-4_____
   Hebrews 12:6-11
d. Ephesians 4:11-13 _____
Circle areas in which you are presently experiencing growth.

3. What are the results of the *Spirit*-filled life (Ephesians 5:18-21)?
   a. _____
   b. _____
   c. _____

4. What are the results of the *Word*-filled life (Colossians 3:16-18)?
   a. _____
   b. _____
   c. _____

5. List all the results of abiding in Christ that you can find in John 15:1-14. Compare Psalm 91. _____
   _____
   _____
   _____

6. Sometimes our very failures or weaknesses become blessings because they make us depend more on God. Share an experience you have had of abiding in Christ recently.

Christian Maturity

7. *Beyond Spiritual Gifts*[1] stresses the importance of

[1]Yohn, Rick, *Beyond Spiritual Gifts* (Wheaton, Ill.: Tyndale House, 1976)

developing mature Christian character. List the fruit which will result when a person is filled and controlled by the Holy Spirit.

a. Galatians 5:22, 23 _____

b. John 4:35, 36 _____

c. Colossians 1:10 _____

Thank God that he is able to develop this fruit in you.

8. Name the process which must take place in order for us to mature spiritually.

a. Galatians 2:20 _____

b. Ephesians 3:16-19 _____

c. Colossians 3:1-3 _____

How has this process been experienced in your life?

9. 1 Corinthians 13:1-3, 13, and Colossians 3:14 emphasize the importance of being controlled by what characteristic? _____

_____

Do you need more of this virtue? Claim Romans 5:5.

10. Bev LaHaye's book, *The Spirit-Controlled Woman*,[2] illustrates the necessity for all women in all walks of life to experience the Spirit-controlled life.

Application

1. Becoming like Christ involves spending time with him (Isaiah 40:31). How much time do you spend each day with him in prayer and Bible study?

2. Are you accepting your trials and problems as one of God's methods of bringing spiritual maturity and growth into your life?

3. Have you asked to be filled with the Holy Spirit? Thank him for this provision.

[2]LaHaye, Beverly, *The Spirit-Controlled Woman* (Irvine, Cal.: Harvest House, 1976)

Prayer

Father, send your Spirit into our hearts so that all of our emotions may be under his control and guidance. And bring us into fruitfulness and spiritual maturity, for the sake of your kingdom. Amen.

Recommended Books

1. Landorf, Joyce, *The Fragrance of Beauty* (Wheaton, Ill.: Victor Books, 1973). Also see the footnotes on Yohn's and LaHaye's books.